Everything Is Beautiful

Everything Is Beautiful

Selected by
Kitty McDonald Clevenger

Hallmark Editions

Everything Is Beautiful

Only that day dawns

to which we are awake.

HENRY DAVID THOREAU

Dee Etta,

*Though we travel the world over
to find the beautiful,
we must carry it with us
or we will find it not.*

RALPH WALDO EMERSON

It is chance that makes brothers,

but hearts that make friends.

VON GEIBEL

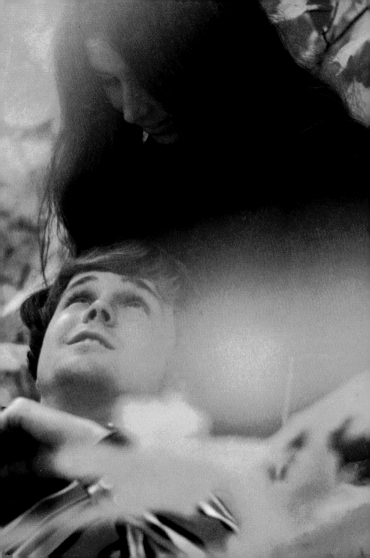

The only way to win happiness
is to give it.
The more we give,
the more we have.

MYRTLE REED

To be curious is to be alive:
To sense the wonder
In things, great and small....

KATHERINE EDELMAN

*The only rose without thorns
is friendship.*

MLLE. DE SCUDERY

Look to this day
for it is life,
the very life of life.

from the SANSKRIT

*Every individual has a place to fill
in the world
and is important,
in some respect,
whether he chooses to be so or not.*

NATHANIEL HAWTHORNE

Kindness is the sunshine
in which virtue grows.

R. G. INGERSOLL

There is a pleasure
in the pathless woods,
There is a rapture
on the lonely shore....

LORD BYRON

Kindness in words creates confidence,
Kindness in thinking
creates profoundness,
Kindness in giving creates love.

LAO-TSE

*Today is the first day
of the rest of your life.*

CHARLES A. DEDERICH

I am not afraid of tomorrow,
for I have seen yesterday
and I love today.

WILLIAM ALLEN WHITE

The heart has its own memory,
        like the mind,
And in it are enshrined
        The precious keepsakes....

HENRY WADSWORTH LONGFELLOW

If we should live a thousand years...
Our time is today, today.

JAMES MONTGOMERY

A friend may well be reckoned

a masterpiece of nature.

RALPH WALDO EMERSON

You will find,

as you look back upon your life,

that the moments that stand out

are the moments

when you have done things for others.

HENRY DRUMMOND

Happiness seems made to be shared.

PIERRE CORNEILLE

*The sun does not shine
for a few trees and flowers,
but for the wide world's joy.*

HENRY WARD BEECHER

For everything there is a season,
and a time for every matter
                              under heaven:
...a time to love, and a time to hate,
a time for war, and a time for peace.

ECCLESIASTES 3:1,8 RSVB

*Life kisses us
on both cheeks day and morn.*

KAHLIL GIBRAN

It's all I have to bring today,
This, and my heart beside,
This, and my heart, and all the fields,
And all the meadows wide....

EMILY DICKINSON

*I would not live
without the love of my friends.*

JOHN KEATS

The greatest use of life
is to spend it for something
that will outlast it.

WILLIAM JAMES

*When one has much to put in them,
a day has a hundred pockets.*

FRIEDRICH NIETZSCHE

The future is not a gift;

it is an achievement.

ROBERT F. KENNEDY

*Very little is needed
to make a happy life.
It is all within yourself,
in your way of thinking.*

MARCUS AURELIUS

*Flowers are the beautiful
hieroglyphics of Nature,
with which she indicates
how much she loves us.*

JOHANN WOLFGANG VON GOETHE

To accomplish great things,
we must not only act but also dream,
not only plan but also believe.

ANATOLE FRANCE

*How beautiful a day can be
when kindness touches it.*

GEORGE ELLISTON

Though I am different

from you,

We were born involved

in one another.

T'AO CH'IEN